Birthday alerts

Playing with his new ph_____tion
that lets him set alerts th_____n
when it's a friend's birth_____ok
for one minute, then turn_____page and till in the missing
dates on the screens. Turn back to check your answers.

NAME	BIRTHDAY
Roopa	November 30th
Matt	April 25th
Freddie	September 6th
Sophia	February 1st
Jordan	June 15th
Ben	April 19th

Birthday alerts

Look at the previous page to find out how to do this puzzle.

Petal pattern

Look at this petal pattern for one minute. Then, turn the page and add the petals that are missing. Turn back to check your answer.

Petal pattern

Look at the previous page to find out how to do this puzzle.

Spotted dogs

Memorize the number of spots on each dog for one minute, then turn the page. See if you can draw the right number of spots on the dogs with plain coats. Turn back to check your answer.

Spotted dogs

Look at the previous page to find out how to do this puzzle.

Packing puzzle

Josie is packing to go on a trip. Memorize the items on her list for one minute, then turn the page to see the things she's going to put in her suitcase. What's missing? Check the list to see if your answer is correct.

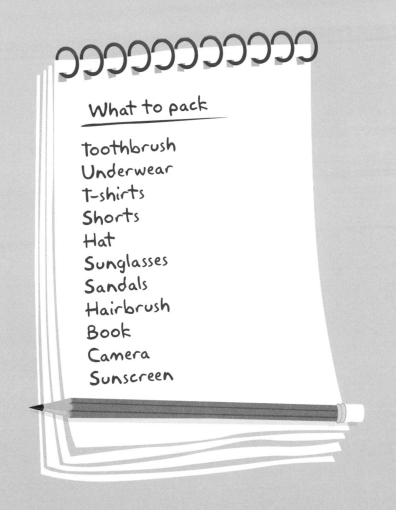

What to pack

Toothbrush
Underwear
T-shirts
Shorts
Hat
Sunglasses
Sandals
Hairbrush
Book
Camera
Sunscreen

Packing puzzle

Look at the previous page to find out how to do this puzzle.

Answers:...

....

Bug finder

Look closely at these bugs for one minute, then turn the page. Can you find them amongst all the other bugs? Turn back to see if you're right.

Bug finder

Look at the previous page to find out how to do this puzzle.

Shark sketch

Look at this picture for one minute, then turn the page.
Can you draw what you've just seen? Turn back to
check your answer.

Shark sketch

Look at the previous page to find out how to do this puzzle.

Dear diary

Here's a torn-out page from an old diary. Read it carefully, then turn the page. Can you circle the things that are mentioned in the diary? Turn back to check your answers.

The huge iron gate swung open and I began to walk slowly up the weed-covered path. As I neared the house, I heard a strange scratching sound. Looking up, I saw the bare branches of an old tree scraping against the shuttered windows of the house as the wind blew.

Taking a deep breath, I crept past the grinning gargoyle statues that guarded the front steps and stood, knees trembling, at the front door. My hand shaking, I reached out for the silver door knocker. It creaked as I slowly lifted it.

Dear diary

Look at the previous page to find out how to do this puzzle.

Seeing circles

Look at this circle pattern for one minute, then turn the page. Can you shade in the missing circles from the pattern? The first few have been done for you. Turn back to see how you did.

Seeing circles

Look at the previous page to find out how to do this puzzle.

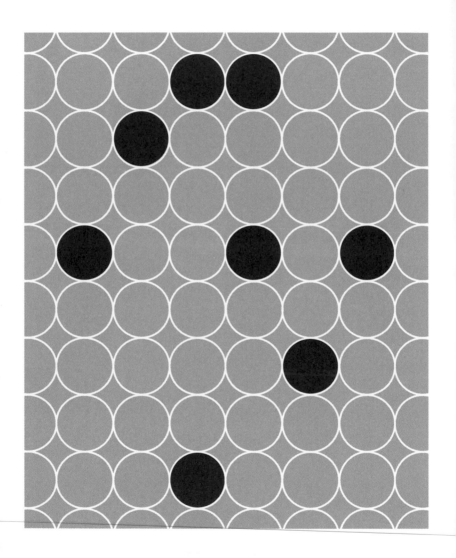

Cats and kittens

Take a look at this scene for one minute, then turn the page and draw circles around **six** things that have changed. Turn back to see if you're right.

Cats and Kittens

Look at the previous page to find out how to do this puzzle.

In uniform

Look at this soldier's uniform for one minute, then turn the page. Can you remember which clothes you saw? Circle the correct items, then turn back to check your answer.

In uniform

Look at the previous page to find out how to do this puzzle.

Ballerinas

Look at these ballerina pictures for one minute, then turn the page. Draw an X by the pictures that are exactly the same as these, then turn back to see if you were right.

Ballerinas

Look at the previous page to find out how to do this puzzle.

Sandwich fillings

Look at this sandwich for 30 seconds, then turn the page.
Number the correct fillings in the order they appear in
the sandwich, from top to bottom. Turn back to see
how you did.

Sandwich fillings

Look at the previous page to find out how to do this puzzle.

Egg

Cheese

Tomatoes

Lettuce

Chicken

Cucumber

Ham

Olives

Carrot

Fishing fun

Look at these people fishing for one minute, then turn the page. Draw lines to connect each fish to the person who caught it. Turn back to check your answers.

Fishing fun

Look at the previous page to find out how to do this puzzle.

Sporty numbers

Look at the numbers on these people's clothes for one minute. Then, turn the page and write the correct number on each person. Turn back to check your answers.

Sporty numbers

Look at the previous page to find out how to do this puzzle.

Cake decorating

Look at the cake for one minute, then turn the page. Can you draw the decorations in the correct places on the plain cake? Turn back to see how you did.

Cake decorating

Look at the previous page to find out how to do this puzzle.

Too many toys

Look at these toys for one minute, then turn the page. There are **two** extra toys on the next page that aren't in the picture below. Draw circles around them, then turn back to see if you're right.

Too many toys

Look at the previous page to find out how to do this puzzle.

Whose lunch?

Look at these lunchboxes for one minute, then turn the page. Can you write the missing names on the correct boxes? Turn back to check your answers.

Whose lunch?

Look at the previous page to find out how to do this puzzle.

Elephant switch

Look at these elephants for one minute, then turn the page. Can you circle the elephants that have switched places? (There should be **four** in all.) Turn back to see if you're right.

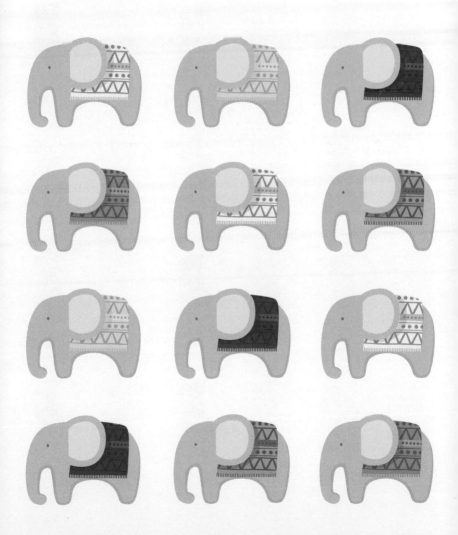

Elephant switch

Look at the previous page to find out how to do this puzzle.

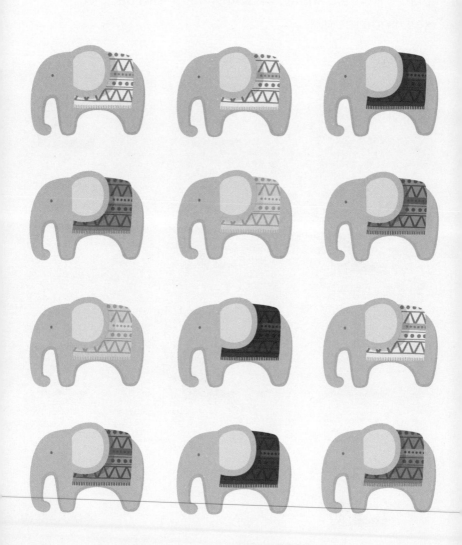

In the charts

30 students were asked what kind of music they liked the most. Take a look at these results, then turn the page. Which of the bar charts shows the right results? Turn back to see if you're correct.

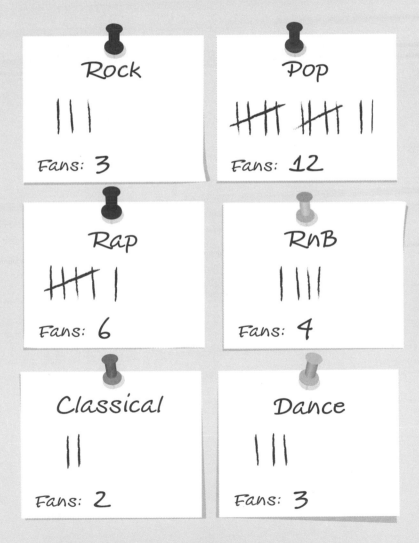

Rock

|||

Fans: 3

Pop

HHT HHT ||

Fans: 12

Rap

HHT |

Fans: 6

RnB

||||

Fans: 4

Classical

||

Fans: 2

Dance

|||

Fans: 3

In the charts

Look at the previous page to find out how to do this puzzle.

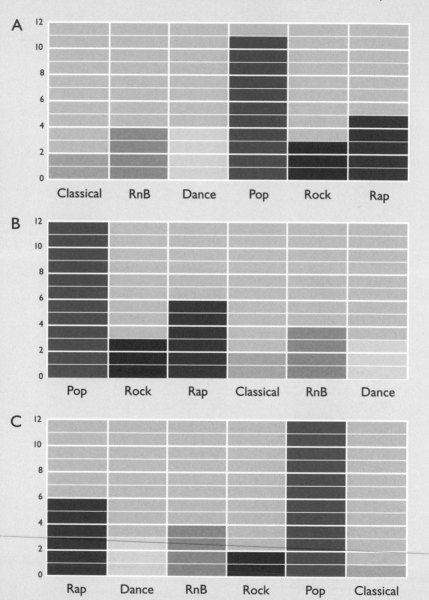

A
Classical RnB Dance Pop Rock Rap

B
Pop Rock Rap Classical RnB Dance

C
Rap Dance RnB Rock Pop Classical

Going shopping

Look at these buildings for one minute, then turn the page. Can you write the names of the businesses next to the items you would find in them? Turn back to check your answers.

Going shopping

Look at the previous page for instructions on how to do this puzzle.

Triangles

Look at this pattern of triangles for one minute, then turn the page. Can you recreate the pattern by filling in the right triangles? The first one has been done for you. Turn back to check your answer.

Triangles

Look at the previous page to find out how to do this puzzle.

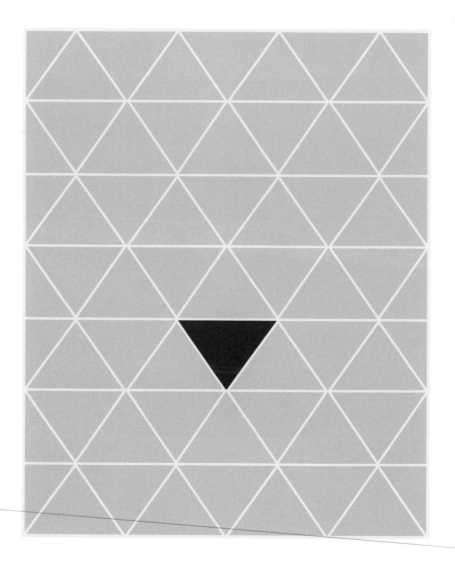

Museum map

Look at this museum map for one minute, then turn the page. Can you draw lines to connect the objects to the right rooms? Turn back to check if you were correct.

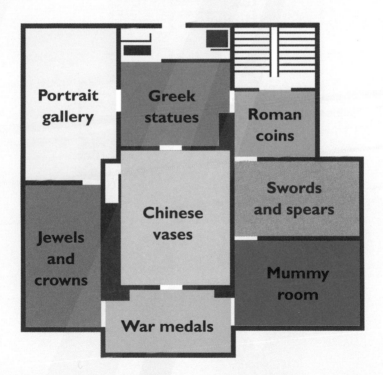

Museum level
(1st Floor)

Portrait gallery

Greek statues

Roman coins

Chinese vases

Swords and spears

Jewels and crowns

Mummy room

War medals

Museum map

Look at the previous page to see how to do this puzzle.

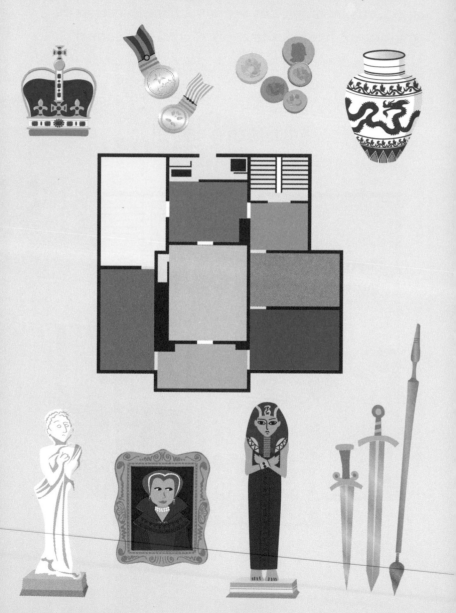

Along the way

Take a minute to look at all the things Daisy passes on the way from her house to Rose's house. Then, turn the page and choose the notebook that lists the things she passes in the correct order. Turn back to check your answer.

Rose's house

Daisy's house

Start

Along the way

Look at the previous page to find out how to do this puzzle.

A

Daisy's house
Cows in a field
Park
Bridge
Woods
House with red door
Windmill
Rose's house

B

Daisy's house
Cows in a field
Park
Bridge
House with red door
Woods
Windmill
Rose's house

C

Daisy's house
Cows in a field
Park
House with red door
Bridge
Woods
Windmill
Rose's house

D

Daisy's house
Cows in a field
Park
House with red door
Woods
Bridge
Windmill
Rose's house

Answer: ....

Ice-cream sundaes

Look at these orders for three ice-cream sundaes for one minute, then turn the page. Draw lines to connect the right ingredients to the correct glasses. Turn back to see how you've done.

Sundae 1

Strawberry ice cream
Chocolate ice cream
Strawberry slices

Sundae 2

Mint ice cream
Chocolate ice cream
Crushed nuts

Sundae 3

Vanilla ice cream
Strawberry ice cream
Whipped cream

Ice-cream sundaes

Look at the previous page for instructions on how to do this puzzle.

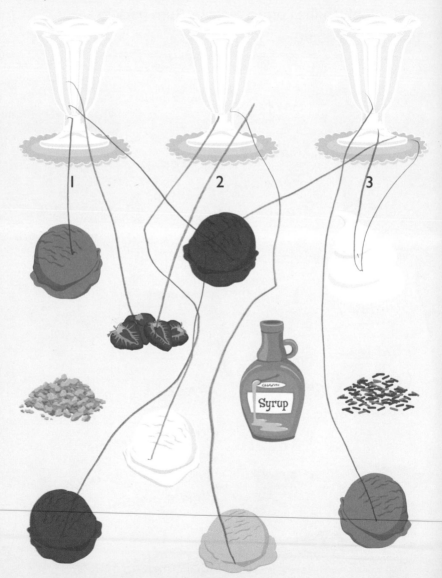

At the aquarium

Joe has been to the aquarium and has seen all the animals in this picture. Look at the picture for one minute, then fill in the missing parts of Joe's report on the next page. Turn back to check your answers.

At the aquarium

Look at the previous page to see how to do this puzzle.

Joe Smith   August 14th

I went to the aquarium today and came

face to face with an enormous....Shark.....

It had lots of teeth! I also saw two

........Seahrose..................., one was green

and the other was blue. There was a group

of bright pink fish, too – there were .....8..........

of them in all. The funniest thing I noticed

was a .....Crab.............

holding onto a turtle's

foot as it swam!

A turtle and two clownfish

Gift list

Look at this list for one minute, then turn the page. Draw lines to match each gift tag to the correct gift. Turn back to see how you did.

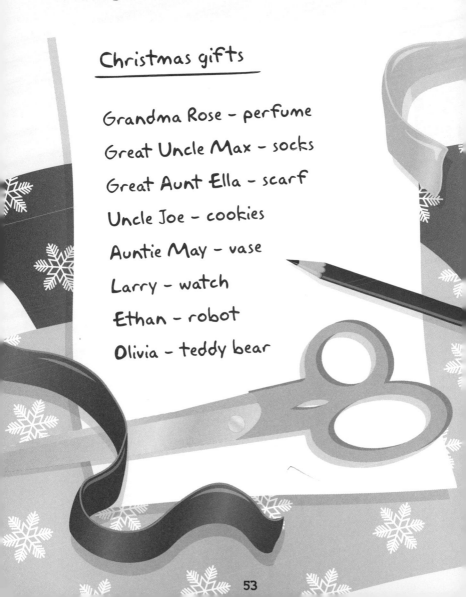

Christmas gifts

Grandma Rose - perfume

Great Uncle Max - socks

Great Aunt Ella - scarf

Uncle Joe - cookies

Auntie May - vase

Larry - watch

Ethan - robot

Olivia - teddy bear

Gift list

Look at the previous page to find out how to do this puzzle.

Racing numbers

Look at these racing cars for one minute, then turn the page. Can you write the correct numbers on the cars? Turn back to see if you're right.

Racing numbers

Look at the previous page to find out how to do this puzzle.

Sky scene

Look at this picture for one minute, then turn the page. Can you circle **five** things that have been added to the scene? Turn back to see how you did.

Sky scene

Look at the previous page to find out how to do this puzzle.

Monster match

Lucas has drawn a picture of the toy monster he would like from the toy store. Look at his sketch for 30 seconds, then turn the page. Can you find the exact monster he has drawn amongst all the other monsters on the shelves?

Monster match

Look at the previous page to find out how to do this puzzle.

Card quiz

Look at these cards for one minute, then turn the page to answer questions about them. When you've completed all the questions, turn back to check your answers.

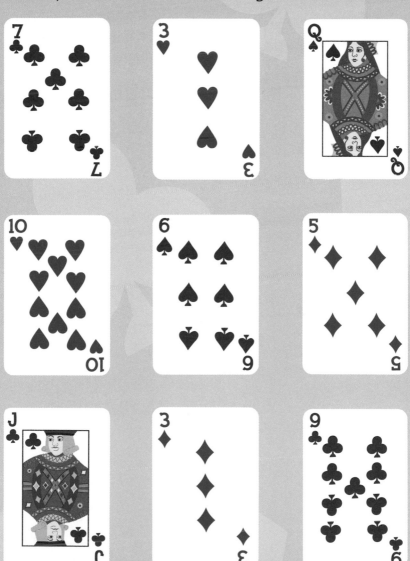

Card quiz

Look at the pictures on the previous page for one minute, then turn back over. Underline the correct answers to the questions below without turning back.

1. Which of these cards was in the middle of the second row?

2. Which of these cards was directly above the five of diamonds?

3. Which of these cards was directly underneath the seven of clubs?

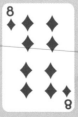  

Star patterns

Look at these three patterns of stars in the night sky for one minute, then turn the page. Can you join the right stars to make the correct patterns? Turn back to see how you did.

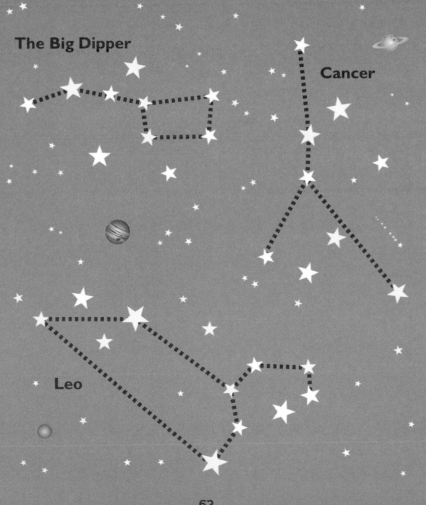

The Big Dipper

Cancer

Leo

Star patterns

Look at the previous page to find out how to do this puzzle.

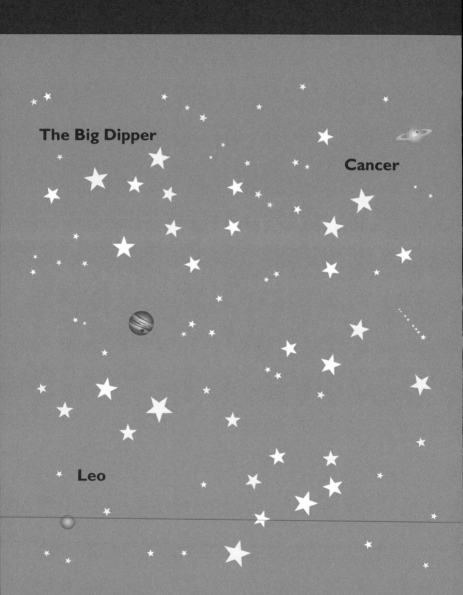

The Big Dipper

Cancer

Leo

Picture postcard

Look at the pictures on this postcard for one minute, then turn the page. Can you circle the **five** differences? Turn back to see if you're right.

Picture postcard

Look at the previous page to find instructions on how to do this postcard puzzle.

Guinea pig puzzle

Look at these guinea pigs for 30 seconds, then turn the page. Can you name the guinea pig that is missing? Turn back to check your answer.

Brownie

Scruff

Nibbles

Patches

Squeaker

Guinea pig puzzle

Look at the previous page to find out how to do this puzzle.

Answer: ....

Yours to mine

Your friend has given you instructions to walk from your house to hers. Look at the directions below for one minute, then turn the page and choose the map that shows the correct route. Turn back to check your answer.

Come out of your house and turn left.

Take the first turn on the right.

My house is the second one on the right.

Yours to mine

Look at the previous page to find out how to do this puzzle.

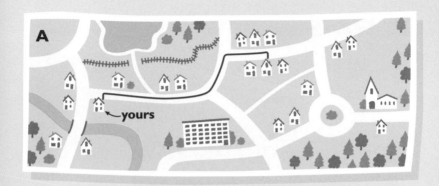

A

yours

B

yours

C

yours

Missing cupcakes

Look at this cake stand of cupcakes for one minute, then turn the page. From the options given, can you circle the **two** cupcakes that have been eaten? Turn back to check your answers.

Missing cupcakes

Look at the previous page to find out how to do this puzzle.

Options:

Under umbrellas

Memorize the umbrellas and the names of the people holding them for one minute, then turn the page. Whose umbrella is missing from the umbrella stand? Turn back to check your answer.

Jilly

Felix

Danny

Tom

Bella

Emma

Under umbrellas

Look at the previous page to find out how to do this puzzle.

Answer: ....

Gift wrapping

Look at these gifts for one minute, then turn the page.
Draw lines to connect each sheet of giftwrap to the
correct present. Turn back to check your answers.

Gift wrapping

Look at the previous page to find out how to do this puzzle.

Coded message

Help Secret Agent Q to find out where some top secret documents have been hidden. Memorize the code below for one minute. Then, turn the page and use what you remember to decode a message between enemy agents. Turn back to check your answer.

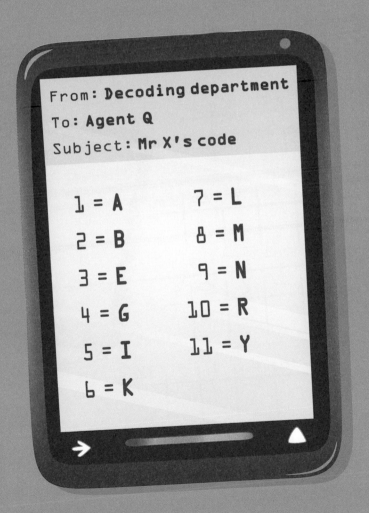

From: **Decoding department**
To: **Agent Q**
Subject: **Mr X's code**

1 = A	7 = L
2 = B	8 = M
3 = E	9 = N
4 = G	10 = R
5 = I	11 = Y
6 = K	

Coded message

Look at the previous page to find out how to do this puzzle.

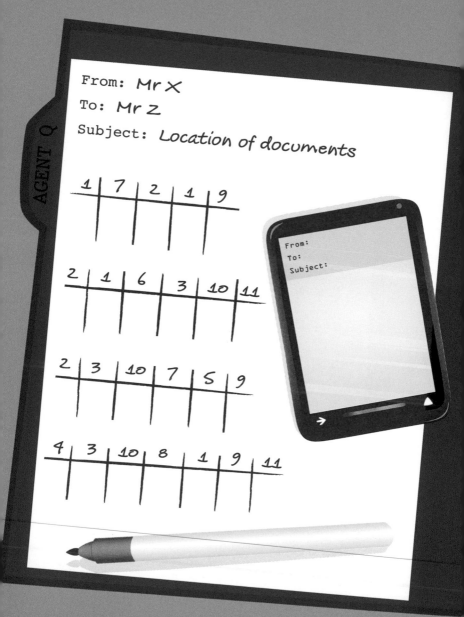

From: Mr X
To: Mr Z
Subject: Location of documents

1	7	2	1	9

2	1	6	3	10	11

2	3	10	7	5	9

4	3	10	8	1	9	11

From:
To:
Subject:

Dinosaur drawing

Look at this picture for one minute, then turn the page.
Can you draw what you've just seen? Turn back to
check your answer.

Dinosaur drawing

Look at the previous page to find out how to do this puzzle.

Pencil cases

Take a look at these pencil cases and their contents for one minute, then turn the page and draw lines to join the items to their correct case. Turn back to see if you're right.

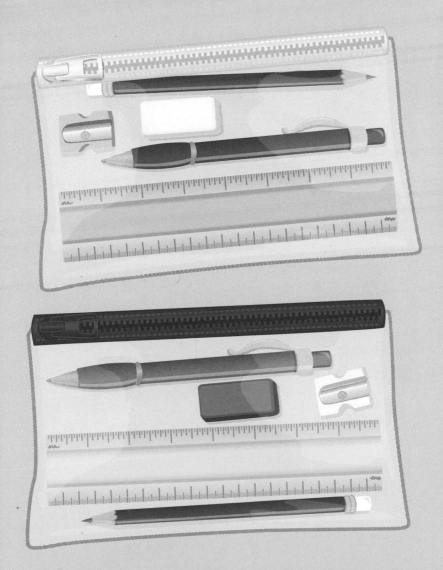

Pencil cases

Look at the previous page to find out how to do this puzzle.

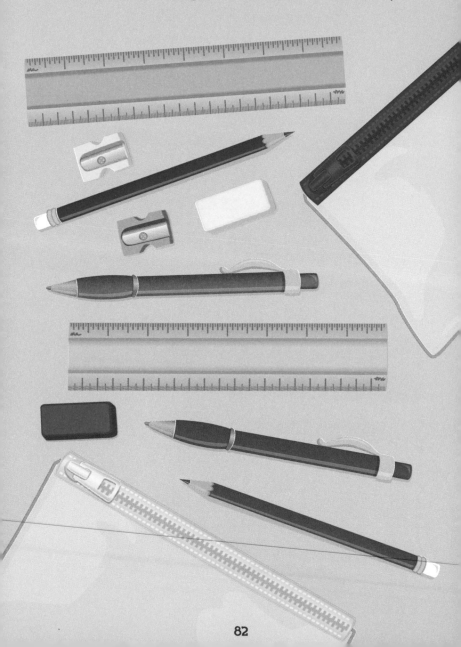

Spelling test

Ollie is learning the ten words below for a spelling test. He memorizes the words in order, then writes them out on a blank sheet of paper. Look at the words for one minute, then turn the page to see Ollie's list. Circle the words that he has changed and that are in the wrong order. Turn back to check your answers.

Spelling List

1. receive
2. difficult
3. occasion
4. rhythm
5. conscience

6. separate
7. leisure
8. principal
9. restaurant
10. embarrass

Spelling test

Look at the previous page to find out how to do this puzzle.

Spellings

1. deceive

2. difficult

3. rhythm

4. occasion

5. conscious

6. separate

7. leisure

8. principle

9. restaurant

10. embarrass

/10

Royal banners

Read the descriptions of these kings' banners for one minute, then turn the page. Can you write the names of the correct kings above their banners? Turn back to see how you did.

KING JEFF

Stripes of red, yellow and blue. Three black stars in yellow stripe.

KING JIM

Stripes of yellow, blue and red. Black star in top corner of yellow stripe.

KING JOHN

Stripes of blue, yellow and red. Green star in middle of yellow stripe.

Royal banners

Look at the previous page to find out how to do this puzzle.

1. ....

2. ....

3. ....

Lost property

Spend one minute memorizing these ten items of lost property, then turn the page. Can you list them all? Turn back to check your answers.

Lost property

Look at the previous page to see how to do this puzzle.

1. ....

2. ....

3. ....

4. ....

5. ....

6. ....

7. ....

8. ....

9. ....

10. ....

Cookie cutters

Look at these cookies for 30 seconds, then turn the page to see some of the cookie cutters that made them. **Two** cookie cutters are missing. Can you draw them in the blank spaces? Turn back to see if you've drawn the right shapes.

Cookie cutters

Look at the previous page to see how to do this puzzle.

Butterfly lives

These pictures show the different stages of life for three butterflies. Memorize them for 30 seconds, then turn the page. Draw arrows joining the different stages for each butterfly. Turn back to see if you're right.

Egg   **Caterpillar**   **Butterfly**

Butterfly lives

Look at the previous page to find out how to do this puzzle.

Squares and symbols

Memorize these squares and their symbols for one minute, then turn the page. Can you draw the correct symbols on the right squares? Some have already been done for you. Turn back to check your answers.

Squares and symbols

Look at the previous page to find out how to do this puzzle.

Robots

Look at these robots for one minute, then turn the page. Are the statements about the different parts of the robots true or false? Underline T or F next to each statement. Turn back to check your answers.

Robots

Look at the previous page to find out how to do this puzzle.

1. The blue robot has a bigger nose than the red robot.
T / F

2. The yellow robot has smaller feet than the red robot.
T / F

3. The blue robot is taller than the red robot. T / F

4. The yellow robot has bigger ears than the blue robot. T / F

5. The red robot has smaller hands than the blue robot.
T / F

6. The yellow robot has longer legs than the red robot.
T / F

Alien solar system

Look at these planets from an alien solar system for one minute, then turn the page. Put the planets in the correct order by writing their numbers next to their names. Turn back to see how you did.

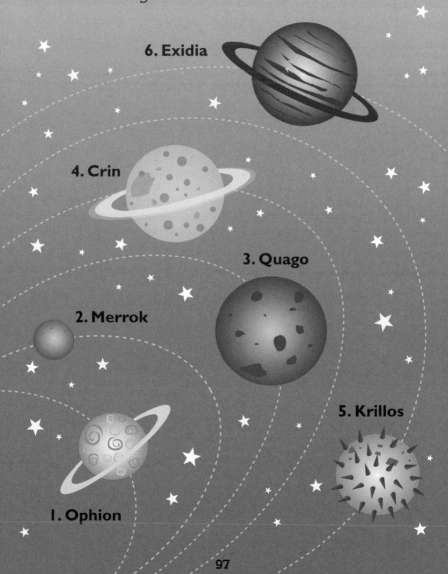

6. Exidia

4. Crin

3. Quago

2. Merrok

5. Krillos

1. Ophion

Alien solar system

Look at the previous page to find out how to do this puzzle.

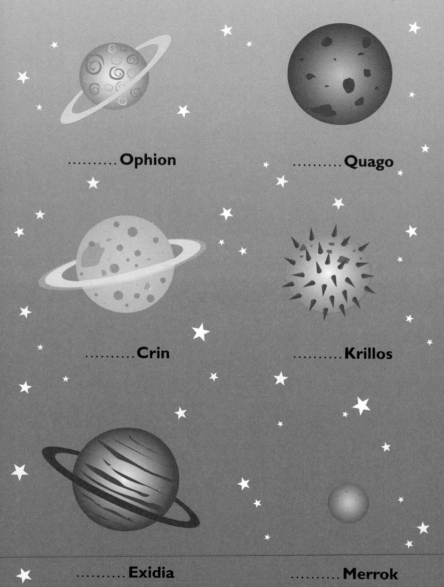

.... **Ophion**

.... **Quago**

.... **Crin**

.... **Krillos**

.... **Exidia**

.... **Merrok**

Block man

Look at this block figure for one minute, then turn the page. Fill in the correct blocks to recreate the figure. Some of the blocks have already been filled in for you. Then, turn back to see how you did.

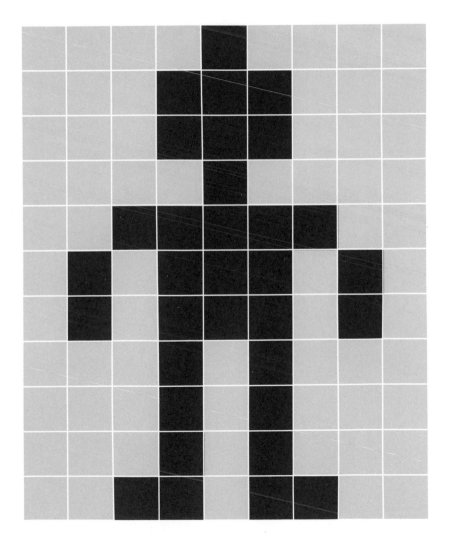

Block man

Look at the previous page to find out how to do this puzzle.

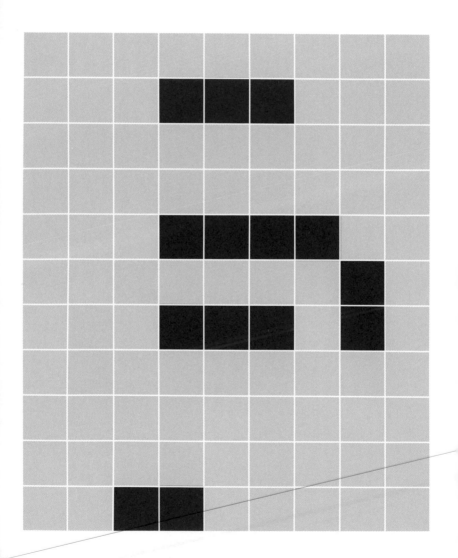

Bird spotting

Take a look at these descriptions of birds for one minute, then turn the page. Write each bird's name next to it, then turn back to check if you're right.

July 3

Light patch on top of head

Red face

Chaffinch

July 5

Linnet

Red patch on forehead

White collar around neck

July 10

Black head

Dark spots on stomach

Brambling

Bird spotting

Look at the previous page to see the instructions on how to do this puzzle.

Penguin picture

Look at this picture for one minute, then turn the page.
Can you draw what you've just seen? Turn back to
check your answer.

Penguin picture

Look at the previous page to find out how to do this puzzle.

On tour

Ironstine, the rock band, are about to start a world tour. Look at the information on their tour T-shirt for one minute, then turn the page and fill in the blanks on their tour poster. Turn back to see if you're right.

WORLD TOUR

IRONSTINE

Oct 23 - New York, USA

Oct 25 - London, UK

Oct 26 - Berlin, Germany

Oct 27 - Paris, France

Nov 01 - Tokyo, Japan

Nov 03 - Sydney, Australia

On tour

Look at the previous page to find out how to do this puzzle.

WORLD TOUR

IRONSTINE

Oct 23   –   _new york_,   **USA**

Oct _25_   –   **London, UK**

Oct 26   –   **Berlin, Germany**

Oct 27   –   _Paris_, _France_

Nov 01   –   **Tokyo, Japan**

Nov _3_   –   **Sydney, Australia**

Balloons

Look at the designs on these balloons for one minute.
Then, turn the page and draw the correct design on each
balloon. Some have been started for you. Turn back to
see how you did.

Balloons

Look at the previous page to find out how to do this puzzle.

Moving marbles

Look at these marbles for one minute, then turn the page.
Can you circle the marbles that have swapped places?
(There should be **six** in all.) Turn back to see if you're right.

Moving marbles

Look at the previous page to find out how to do this puzzle.

Finding fish

Look closely at these fish for one minute, then turn the page. Can you find them and circle them amongst all the other fish? Turn back to see if you're right.

Finding fish

Look at the previous page to find out how to do this puzzle.

Written by Sarah Khan.
Designed by Kate Rimmer, Michael Hill and Ruth Russell.
Illustrated by Lizzie Barber and Non Figg.

First published in 2014 by Usborne Publishing Ltd, 83–85 Saffron Hill, London ECIN 8RT, England.